Snaps with his teeth that shaft of deadly gall,
And grinds with foam and blood the sputtered splinters small.
Turned to the rescued maid, along the brow
Of Torthil lightens a heroic smile;
Till, o'er his drained benumbed limb forced to bow,
To earth succumbs he, gazing yet the while
On her whose presence can his pains beguile.

But she for him her silken vesture tears,
Binds his stanched wound with pity's gentlest wile;
Cold sprinklings then from out the stream she bears,
Refreshes his sick face, his fainting strength repairs.
"And spare," he said, "for me those wistful fears.
Wonder divine! thee in a dream of yore
Twice did I see—mine own! Not years, long years,
Could make me know, could make me love thee more.
My heart's last blood I'd give thee o'er and o'er!
I would but have thee know me should I die:
Afar I come from Caledonia's shore,
Torthil my name, a chieftain there was I;
A captive next—nay, sent thy safety thus to buy
"I am a savage; but in thy sweet sight
To live, would make me gentle soon, and wise.
Would thou couldst love me!" With impassioned might
He strove, nor vainly, from the ground to rise.
The light was thickened in his heavy eyes;
He fell, yet falling kissed her dear young feet.
Alone the fainting Caledonian lies,
The maid in haste has sought the wood's retreat;
But soon she reappears with new assistance meet.
A reverend father and a female old
Come to her guidance, and the youth upraise;
His drooping head the virgin's hands uphold:
Borne o'er the rivulet, through the woodland maze,
Where many a path the uncertain foot betrays,
A cave withdrawn into the mountain's side,
Received them from the forest's puzzling ways.
There Father Hippo healing bands supplied;
And there, till he wax well, young Torthil shall abide.

But oft Roscrana came, that Princess good,
Niece of Zenobia, Tadmor's famous Queen,
Who, since Aurelian had her throne subdued,
With honour placed in Italy had been.
A huntress, she her summer dwelling green
Chose near the central mountains of the land.
Fair daughters round her graced the sylvan scene;
But she, and they, a haughty sister-band,

Roscrana's meekness scorned, and ruled her with high hand.
Yet more divided from her kindred blood,
Roscrana's heart confessed our holy faith;
Nursed by a Christian Jewess, and imbued
With early love for Him of Nazareth,
She to His Cross will cling unto the death.
The sovereign knowledge fain would she declare
To her proud kin, but still they shunned her path;
Then sought she solace in the woods, and there
She found the cave proscribed of that old Christian pair.
They o'er the Syrian orphan, as their child,
Rejoiced, that dear faith mutually confessed.
More than a daughter, she their fears beguiled,
She brought them food, she watched their aged rest,
Fit garments wrought by her their bodies dressed.
For this, the scrolls of the Eternal Word
Given by those saints, she hid beneath her vest,
Till to the night, to shady walks restored,
She drew them forth and read of her incarnate Lord.
Within the cavern of those Christians laid,
With plants of healing gathered from the hill,
Was Torthil cured by that Palmyran maid,
Oh more to love her for her gentle skill.

And soon he blessed those days of wounded ill,
For aye young pity trembles into love;
Lord of her heart is he and virgin will.
And aye to him of Jesus from above
She reads, or in the cave, or walking through the grove.
Sequestered they in love's unworldly dream,
In haunts of beauty lose the lapsing hours.
Forth by the lake, down by the living stream,
They dip their footsteps in the dewy flowers.
The glad birds twinkle from their morning bowers.
Noon's sultry silence on the forest broods.
Eve flushes soft: clear glance the sunny showers:
The mountains smile with all their hanging woods:
Lustre in all the vales, lustre on all the floods!
The stock-dove's voice, sweet intermittent bird,
That aye the shadow of the hawk's wing fears,
Crushed in the depth of leaves, and faintly heard,
Moaning of love, the twilight hour endears
To the young lovers. Lo! the Moon appears;
Beauty and Peace lead on the silver Queen;
The forests, brightening silently, she clears;
She walks the mountains; o'er the polished sheen
Of dimpling rivers far her sliding feet are seen.
Another eve: turned to the lord of day,

The Christian Bride & The Churchyard by Thomas Aird

Thomas Aird was born on 28th August 1802 at Bowden, Roxburghshire in Scotland.

After an education at the local parish school he studied for his degree at Edinburgh University. Whilst there he became friends with fellow writers James Hogg, Thomas Carlyle and John Wilson.

After graduating Aird was encouraged to become a Church of Scotland minister but he turned down these entreaties to remain in Edinburgh and devote himself to a literary career.

His first publication was in 1826 with 'Martzoufle: A Tragedy in Three Acts, with other Poems', unfortunately the collection received little attention from either critics or the public.

Aird was a regular contributor to Blackwood's Magazine and among other works a series of essays entitled 'Religious Characteristics'.

He was best known for his narrative poem 'The Captive of Fez' which was published in 1830 to a far better and wider reception.

Between 1832 and 1833, Aird succeeded James Ballantyne as the editor of the Edinburgh Weekly Journal. From 1835, he became the editor of the Dumfriesshire and Galloway Herald, a post he then held for the next 28 years. While editor, several of his poems were published within its pages.

1848, he published a collection of his poetry, 'The Old Bachelor in the Old Scottish Village', which was very well received. His friend, the essayist Thomas Carlyle, said that in his poetry he found "a healthy breath as of mountain breezes."

His last published literary work was his editing of the works of David Macbeth Moir, a physician and writer, in 1852.

Aird was to now concentrate on the editorship of the Herald until he retired in 1863.

Thomas Aird died on 25th April 1876 in Castlebank, Dumfries at the age of 73. He was buried at St Michael's Church.

Index of Contents

THE CHRISTIAN BRIDE

Part First

Young Torthil sits below the woody steeps
Of Apennine, beneath a spreading oak.
His downcast eye a stern abstraction keeps;
Dawn not for him with purple stains has broke,
Nor sunshine filled the world: the captive's yoke
Is on his heart—bright things are not for him.
The cloudy day, the high-winged tempest's shock
Would more delight him, with unbounded limb
Swift o'er far Morven's hills, throughout her forests dim.
Who knows not Torthil from Ausonia's bound
Of Alps Helvetian to her southern heel?
Now homeward musing o'er the vast profound,
The fisher sees him by the ocean kneel;
Now o'er the mountains with impetuous zeal
He strikes the tusky monster with his spear;
The chamois leaps, the bird in airy wheel
Screams to his piercing arrow: far and near,
Scorning a life in Rome, he takes the wild severe.
There Torthil sits. Up looking now he sees
A damsel reading, shaded from the heat,
Beautiful, walking in the myrtle-trees
On yonder bank, forth now in sunlight sweet,
Now glimmering back into the shy retreat
Of twilight green. But hark! adown the vale
A tumult comes, the wild boar gallops fleet,
Two dogs close track him grinning to assail.
Far echoes tell the pack are on some other trail.
Fled has the damsel. Torthil's o'er the brook.
Behind she hears the panting brute advance,
Nearer, and nearer still; she turns to look—
O terror! joy! her eye's bewildered trance
Hangs crowded thick with death and life at once:
The monster's sidelong, half-upturning head
Is gnarled to strike, his bared tusks backward glance
To gather fury for his onset dread,
To tear her tender limb—bold Torthil's lance has sped.
But ah! he stumbles from his forceful blow;
The beast transfixed, disdaining yet to fly,
Has bowed his levelled head, and, ploughing low
As if to pass his rising enemy,
With tearing side-stroke rips his spouting thigh;
Then forward staggers, darkly crushed to fall;
But bites his fiery wound ere he will die,

"So sinks," said Torthil, "the immortal flame.
I too go down: back takes he on his way
His retrospect; if I should do the same,
Pride overthrown, youth crushed, the baffled aim,
Defeat, and exile from my native shore,
Are my memorials—felt by me, for shame
Was never in my father's house; yet sore
Though be my pangs for these, my country plagues me more.

"For me her youth into the battle's waste
She poured, she perished at my sole command.
Was this not much? Am I not all disgraced?
The exulting rivers of my native land,
These are not they—a captive here I stand.
Why fell I not? Yea, farther hear my shame:—
Lady, I chose to stoop beneath their band
Which binds me by the honour of my name,
Since slain not here in Rome, my freedom ne'er to claim,

"Ne'er to attempt return. Oh, I might say,
My very wish that shame to uncreate
Forbade my death, throughout the slavish day
Of circumstances bade me tamely wait
Some better morn of fortune or of fate.
What then? Unbounded blame is still my due
For you betrothed to my forlorn estate.
'Tis time to question thus myself for you,—
What hope contrive, sweet maid, what plan shall I pursue?

"This I might do—Oh, I no more can live
For thee to see me in my slavery!—
Yes, I will do it—I will go—will give
My life again from vows to be set free;
They gall me so! His slave I will not be;
I'll go, I'll brave him on his Roman throne.
Ha! first I'll promise to mine enemy
Long years of service in his battles done;
For thee with power fulfilled, he'll let me then be gone.

"Then home with me to Morven shalt thou go,
And be a daughter to my mother there.
There forth I'll lead thee by the hand, and show
The green translucent brine, when mermaids rare
Chant on the rocks and comb their slippery hair;
The bliss of morn, clear wells, and forests green;
The pure suffusion of the evening air,
When dipped in delicate lights far hills are seen.
Bards with their stately songs shall close our day serene.

"Ha! idle visions these! Why am I here?
Sweet Lady, come with me unto our cave;
Then home I'll guide thee. Ere next noon appear,

Aurelian hears me; wise, and just, and brave,
He'll grant the death of freedom that I crave.
Oh, not in vain last night in dreams did come
To me my mother, pale as from the grave;
Yet smiled the vested image from her home
O'er the wan waters far, over the travelled foam."
Within the cave they wait the evening star.
But came Zenobia, beautifully keen;
Behind her thronging entered men of war;
A Jewish dwarf, misshapen, ugly, lean,
Who long her servant in the East had been,
Led on the party: he, of Christ the foe,
Had learned Roscrana's faith, had brought his Queen
Her doubtful haunt, her friends proscribed to know.
O'erpowered now must they all before Aurelian go.
Yea, worse than vain was Torthil's manly haste
His name to tell, his passion to declare;
Vain priestly Hippo's act, before them placed,
To wed Roscrana to her Torthil there.
Joy then be with them, a divided pair!
The Imperial lady with a deadly smile
Swore (for the Cæsar ne'er denies her prayer)
Dark dungeon chains shall Torthil have the while,
Roscrana banished be to some far foreign isle.

Part Second

In Morven's woody land, Roscrana kissed
Her Torthil's mother at her tale amazed;
Then lowly bowed the virgin to be blest:
"My far-come daughter!" Cathla said, and raised,
And still with wonder on the lady gazed,
"If thou indeed art Torthil's chosen bride;
Yea, well that forehead's beauty undebased
Beseems the scion of a Prince's side:
Worthy art thou to be my Torthil's spouse of pride.
"Thou from the dowried kingdoms of the East,
To lands of poor but of heroic men
Art come; yet court nor oriental feast
Will make thy sweet soul scorn our humblest den.
But when great wars befall, my daughter then
Shall bless the safety that wild Morven yields;
Then shall her sons, from mountain and from glen,
Hang round about thee with their sounding shields:
They for young Torthil's bride would fight a hundred fields."
Forth came the day-spring: forth with Cathla walked

In sleepless love Roscrana from her door.

Before the gate a grizzly giant stalked,
A rough dog gambolled on the grassy floor.
Near stepped the former, this his play gave o'er.
"Behold thy keepers," Cathla said, and smiled:
"Here Rumal, Torthil's hound, feared of the boar;
There silent Erc, who knows each mountain wild:
Where'er inclined to roam, they'll guard my Syrian child.
"One daughter Erc, young Oina-Morul, had,
The white-armed gladdener of his heart and eyes;
She crossed a bridging tree, the torrent mad
Devoured her beauty, stumbling from surprise.
My Torthil sees her, down the bank he flies,
Dash through the whirls he rides the roaring wave,
Green boiling gulf and dull black pool he tries;
Ah! to his sight a filmy whiteness gave
The virgin, only won to a more honoured grave.
"Erc loved my boy, he fought for him, he fell;
Healed by my care, his life from death was won
To be my dragon and to guard me well:
For you how gladly shall the same be done!
Far to the peaks of mountains does he run,
O'er lake below, o'er river, wood, and plain,
He casts his eagle eye to ken my son;
He hies to the wild margin of the main,
To look for the white ships—for Torthil back again."
On mountain-tops when morning lights appear,
When silent dewdrops through the eve distil,
Or by the rising moon, or Hesper clear,
Or when the gusts of gloomier twilight fill
Old creaking thorn upon the stony hill,

Erc, brave and modest, was Roscrana's guide,
The shaggy Rumal was beside him still;
With them the Princess every fear defied,
As over Morven's land she loved to wander wide.
The great north-winds that on the pine-woods blow,
And heave the ocean's elemental floor,
Toss her dark locks that through them boldly go,
Sublime her spirit with their stormy roar.
Heroic land! she loved thee more and more,
Fair, but still roughening to her young surprise;
On heaths she met, and on the awful shore,
Majestic men who looked unto the skies,
For never slavery bowed their unpolluted eyes.
And Cathla told her of her father-land,
The deeds of Fingal, his illustrious race,

The songs of Ossian, the bards' priestly band,
The ghosts of heroes, and their dwelling-place:
They oft, when laid within the desert's space
Their sons have slept beneath the moon's wan beams
By the gray Stone of Power, before them trace
Events to come, vouchsafing them in dreams
Prefiguring gestures stern, soft monitory gleams.
But sad are they that want the funeral-song;
Their spirits mount not to the airy hall
Of eddying winds, for ever rolled along
By weedy lakes within their misty pall.
Of signs she told, of showers of blood that fall
To gifted eyes, the Druid's shuddering grove,
The twangs of death that in the harp-strings call,
The attendant Genii on the maids they love;
And of the Culdees told in many a rocky cove.

And much she loved to hear Roscrana tell
Of all the wonders of the early East.
But who are they that in those caverns dwell?
Each hoary Culdee is a Christian priest.
Roscrana knew them, nor the Princess ceased
Till, more than eloquent, till, saintly bold,
Of Christ, and of her love for Him increased
In this her exile—nay, her home—she told;
Till Cathla wept glad tears, won to The Living Fold.
"Awake, my Christian child!"—by this sweet name
Cathla now named her, as for Torthil's sake
She ever sleepless, when the morning came,
Longed for Roscrana—"My true daughter, wake!
Forth let us go and walk by bower and brake.
Alas! in tears those eyes of beauty swim:
Thee far from me thy nightly visions take,
Far to thy buried mother, far to him
Thy princely sire who sleeps in Tadmor's aisles so dim.
"Or when thy spirit, winged with ghostly dreams,
Flies through the pale dominions of the night,
Thou meet'st thy Torthil by the midnight gleams.
Thou wak'st, and I alone am in thy sight.
Oft wilt thou sigh when comes the morrow bright;
Long wilt thou look unto the East by day
(There were the kingdoms of thy young delight),
Weeping to feel thyself too far away,
Doomed with thy father's dust not even thy dust to lay.
"Weep not, my child! True daughter unto me!
Marvellous blessing to my end of days!
Christ send our Torthil home to us that he
May learn the truth, may learn the Eternal ways!

Then, if redeemed, shall we not be thy praise,
Immortal creature! who hast given us up
To dwell with God, His glory to upraise?
Perish the Druid's fable! the true cup
Of life alone is theirs who with the Lamb shall sup."
And aye with Cathla forth that daughter went,
Grief-silent Erc and Rumal still behind;
Their steps they to the blameless people bent,
Dwelling upon the mountains unconfined,
With peace the broken spirit to upbind,
Want from the poor and sickness to repel.
So meek their Torthil's wife, so sweetly kind,
Gray fathers bade their daughters thus excel,
The mothers called her good, the maidens loved her well.
Too much by Swarno loved, impure of heart,
Her Torthil's foe, he tempted her with sighs;
But true her faith, and vain the chieftain's art,
He with his friend in every enterprise,
The red Gurthullin, did a plot devise:—
Near grows a struggle with the Roman foe
(Succumb shall Morven, or shall greater rise),
The battle o'er, abroad while stragglers go,
They'll watch, they'll bear her off, and none their guilt shall know.
Yea, chastely modest, boldly innocent,
Ne'er has she hinted Swarno's love impure;
Hence ne'er her friends shall guess the way she went:—
"But ha! old dragon Erc must we secure;
Chained must he be, our scheme were else unsure:
Thus be it done,—upon the battle-eve
Him to our nearest fortalice we'll lure;
Rumal his dog we'll slay, and him we'll leave
There fettered till we teach the damsel not to grieve."

Part Third

Forth Cathla went, Roscrana by her side.
But now they heard—the air was all so still—
Trumpet and horn beyond the mountains wide.
The shouts of battle, as they climb the hill,
With hope and fear their panting bosoms fill.
Yon valley now! Their eyes how eager bent!
O day of safety, or of endless ill!
There toils the war of peoples fiercely pent,
O'erstifled, staggering, swayed, with rifts of havoc rent.
The numerous weight of her Imperial foes

O'erbears at length and crushes Morven back,
Eastward away her fainting battle goes;
Their closer forms the o'ermastered horse unslack,
They flee, the skirting mountains wide they track;
The abandoned chariots with unmanaged steeds
Roll mad about, and tear the harrowed rack
Of infantry that to the sheer scythe bleeds,
Wrapping the cloyed wheels round with torn limbs as with weeds.
But lo yon Champion! on he brings anew
The mountain men. The Romans unsustained
Are whelmed in turn. How terrible and true,
The bloody push of Morven is maintained!
Back-rattling chariots have the flight disdained;
They roll around the outskirts of the fight,
Which onward struggles through the field regained.

But o'er them falls the thunder-cloud, like night,
Down on the battle falls, and hides it from the sight.
"Lean on me, mother, to the Culdee's rock,"
Roscrana said, "not distant by the wave,
For friendly shelter from the stormy shock.
By moon, or dawn-light, issuing from his cave,
Our noble wounded let us help to save.
Would Erc were here thee in his arms to bear!
Why has he left us thus? Not he, though brave,
Rolled back the battle: No: that Champion's air
None but a Prince could show: be sure a Prince was there."
They reached the cell. O'erwearied with the day,
Within an inner cavern Cathla slept.
Before the embers as reclined he lay,
The bliss of slumber o'er the Culdee crept.
Alone her vigil young Roscrana kept;
That Champion still in her recurring thought,
She generous tears of admiration wept.
But now the storm was lulled or heard remote;
Forth by the crescent moon the freshening air she sought.
Rough men have seized her: through the forest's skirt
They bear her off. Casting red light before,
What tumult comes? Forth bursts, with shapes begirt,
A stately savage on the woody floor:
'Tis Erc! aloft his pinioned arms he bore,
Unheld to keep them from that galling throng;
Blazed his wild hair; his bleeding loins were sore
With hanging dogs, deep dragged by him along;
Torch-bearing serfs behind strike at the giant strong.

Still on the encumbered warrior draws his trail
Of death and danger to the Princess near;

Her arms to him, to him her face so pale
Imploring stretched, mighty for one so dear
He turns, he sweeps obstruction from his rear;
Bounding he comes; and round Gurthullin's throat,
Who chiefly holds her, wraps his chains severe;
Then wide apart and high his wrists he shot,
And hanged the uplifted wretch, who now his prey forgot.
With starting eyeballs, and self-bitten tongue,
Erc to the ground has dashed the caitiff base.
He snatched the maid; as to his neck she clung,
A smile of daring lit his fire-scarred face.
With her he waded through the thickening chase,
Still dashing off the war that on him hung;
Then down he set her; in the embattled place
There as she stood, away from her he flung
Her circling foes, around so lion-like he sprung.
Before her now o'erwhelmed he's on his knee,
Yet fighting still; a near horn blew a blast;
Forth leapt a haughty figure, followed he
By swift retainers, round his glance he cast,
He saw Roscrana and he seized her fast.
Upsprung, with power indignantly renewed,
Old Erc, a groan from out his large heart passed
To see the maid by Swarno's grasp subdued;
Staggering he clutched the chief who bore her through the wood.
A trumpet blows behind. They turn to see
That coming party whether friends or foes.

Them has Roscrana seen—'tis he! 'tis he!
The chosen hero of that day she knows:
A valiant band around their leader close:
Salvation's near:—"Save! save me, helper true!
Prince Torthil's wife am I; this Swarno knows,
Yet here he"—"But will I not rescue you,
My own good Syrian wife?" And forth her Torthil flew.
Quick with his blade away has Swarno shorn
His black curls gripped by Erc; down on the ground
He set the maid behind him; bold of scorn
And hate he met his foeman with a bound.
Steel they to steel now face each other round,
Lit by the torches; Swarno quits him well,
But Torthil's thrusts his strength and skill confound:
That stroke shall hew him down—ha! stumbling fell
The youth, and o'er him rose fierce Swarno's sword and yell.
Down—ne'er he smote: Erc, sunk with wounds, has crept,
And pulled him backward from his lifted blow,
Struggling to earth; then on his breast he leapt,
And choked with grappling hands the throttled foe;

Recovered Torthil guards old Erc below;
Dread dins the mingled conflict of the rest;
But Swarno slain, his men soon vanquished go.
With danger past and present joy oppressed,
Roscrana, left unhurt, faints on her husband's breast.

With oaken leaves fresh dripping from the rain
Her brow he sprinkles, and she soon revives.
"Joy! joy!" she said, "my hero is not slain!
But where is Erc, the saviour of our lives?"
Near borne he comes; if dying, he derives
Solace from friends so many and so dear:
Each gallant youth to share the burden strives
Of him who trained them to the bow and spear,
They carry him like sons, the brave old man they cheer.
"Heroic creature! To the cave away,"
Roscrana murmured, "of the Culdee John;
There rests my Torthil's mother, since to-day
She saw the great deed of her son unknown:
Sweetly she sleeps upon the rushes strewn;
But sweeter far shall her awaking be.
My Torthil, come! Soft bear the old man on,
The hermit's rocky fastness soon we'll see;
There, ever-faithful Erc, shalt thou be healed by me."
Nor in her thankful joy did she refrain,
But stooping down the old Barbarian kissed;
His heart's best fire, unquenched by fear or pain,
Sprung to his eye, dimmed now with grateful mist;
With clapping hands her love he mutely blessed.
"Now swiftly, gently on with him," she said;
"Deeply though hurt, greatly though needing rest,
His frame's yet full of life; and watchful aid
Shall heal him soon in John's mild sanctuary laid."
"Come then, my Syrian, to our mother fast,"
Her Torthil said, "and fear for me no more:
Here am I with you all your own at last,
My limbs unfettered, and my exile o'er.
Nor I dishonoured left the Italian shore:
Aurelian slain, my friend just Tacitus
Imperial sate, and loosed my bondage sore;
Ennobling freedom has he given to us.
I came; our battle fled, and back I won it thus.

"A grateful vassal of that Swarno slain,
Whose only daughter was to health restored,
And taught God's Word by thee, and who again
Was taught by her the heart-renewing Word,
Heard of this plot against thee by his lord,

And helped from Swarno's dungeon Erc the brave,
Then left for aye the master he abhorred,
And sought me when the fight was o'er, and gave
Hints how to mar the plot—my own dear wife to save.
"Oh how I hasted, hasting still the more,
When I was told that serfs and dogs of blood
Were after Erc, whose flight was known before
He gained the safe recesses of the wood.
Directed well, and glorying in thy good,
Nor dogs nor serfs could stay his strong career;
Though manacled, though felly thus pursued,
He sped to trace, to reach, to save thee here.
And I have found thee too: So be thou of good cheer!
"Nor fear thy holy lessons have been vain:
Blest be my dungeon's leisure to retrace
Thy words of life again and yet again,
Blent in my heart with the remembered grace
Which more than beautified thy saintly face.
Thy faith exalted thus I've won and tried."
But now they reached the Culdee's dwelling-place.
A mother's heart, a son's was satisfied.
Then turned their mingled love to Torthil's Christian Bride.

THE CHURCHYARD

Night The First

With a quick imperfect shriek,
Rose the thin embodied reek.
Like a thing pursued, it fled
From the kingdoms of the dead,
Through the green silent vales
(As the moon unclouded sails),
O'er the dewy-hazèd hill,
Through the forest deep and still,
By the river's sandy shore,
By the gray cliffs gleaming hoar,
Through the fens, and through the floods
Of the fruitless solitudes,
Far to flee through night away
To the healthful coasts of day.
Back shuddering, shimmering, o'er its grave it sate;
Another ghost was near, and thus they mourned their fate:—

FIRST GHOST
O dim unbodied land!

Joy dwells not there, even pain is at a stand.
A smothering presence fills the air around
Of patience dumb, and fears without a sound.

SECOND GHOST

The Heavenly Watchers where,
That deigned for man to cleave the morning air,
And stooping closed, glad message to fulfil,
Their golden wings on many a glorious hill;
And in earth's green and patriarchal days
With converse joyed our fathers' hearts to raise,
Beneath broad tented trees, blessing their state
With great approval, interdiction great?

FIRST GHOST

Far other state is ours! No simple grace
Of life primeval, no green dwelling-place!
Sun there, nor moon, nor ether molten blue,
Valley, nor tufted hill divides the view,
Nor lucid river, on whose borders blow
Flowers many-hued, and trees of stature grow:
Nor leafy summer, nor the stormy glee
Of winds, when winter falls upon the sea,
With change delights us: nor returning morn,
Nor face of man relieves that sad sojourn.

SECOND GHOST

Were men but wise! Did but Ambition know
The flat endurance of our listless wo,
How to his soul would triumph be denied,
How slacked the spasms of his o'ertorturing pride,
Spun from the baffled heart! Oh, how would fail,
Fires of blood and Passions pale!

FIRST GHOST

Behold the goodly pattern of yon heaven!
Beneath yon moon becalmed the woodlands lie.
By dogs of chase the desert creature driven,
Climbs up the rocky stairs of mountains high;
With sealing light she touches his wild eye,
And all the bliss of slumber is for him.
So sweet yon moon to earth! Sweeter to me
Life fresh of blood would be;
'Twould fill my heart with joy up to the trembling brim.

SECOND GHOST

What though the churchyard, by the glimmering light,
Pours forth the empty children of the night;

O'er seas and lands we flit, but back are fain
To troop dishonoured to our place again.
Vain privilege! it serves us but to show
The joy that we for ever must forego.

FIRST GHOST
O the glad earth! no more, ah! never, there
With chaste clear eyes we'll drink the morning air,
Breathed through the sweet green saplings of the spring,
Fresh by the water-courses flourishing!
No more from cooling shades, at noon of day,
We'll watch the crystal waters slide away;
Till come still evening with her drops of dew,
And her large melting moon hung in the southern blue!

SECOND GHOST
From out the west a haze of thick fine rain
Comes o'er green height, high rock, and smoking plain,
Flies lightly drifted o'er the dimmèd floods,
And shakes its sifted veil upon the woods.
Forth looks the sun, the impearled valley fills
With seeds of light, and sleeks the slippery hills.
Nor yet the showery drops away have ceased
To fall, clear glancing on the darkened east,
When o'er them cast, with saffron horns the Bow
Of Beauty melts the fluid woods below.
With glittering heads, down in the grassy plain
The milk-white herds feed onward in a train;
Sheep nibbling up, goats on the higher slopes,
The shepherds stand upon the mountain-tops.
O beauty! O the glory of the hour!
What living spirit could resist your power?
Not mine; far less it could when rustling through
The crimped translucent cups of leaves, with dew
And sunshine overflown, my love first stood in view.
What tranquil might upon that forehead lies!
How pure the spirit that refines those eyes!
Joy dwelt in her, as light dwells in the stone,
Dear to my heart, but now for ever gone.
God, do but clear her from the grave's foul stains,
Pour back the branching blood along her veins,
Build up that lovely head! Oh let her rise,
Let youth's fine light revive within her eyes!

FIRST GHOST
Forks of fire, heaven's floodgates pouring,
Crushed and jammed the thunders roaring,
My bride of beauty by my side

Shrinking, we were touched—and died!
What means this death? O God upon Thy throne,
Give us the day; we'll let Thee not alone!
From floods, and fields, and ways, arise, ye ghosts,
Tribes of dusk time! kingdoms! unnumbered hosts!
No more of sufferance! upward let us flee
To God's own gates, and pray the end to be.
Why fear the light? Why fear the morning air?
Fill we His skies with shrieks, and he must hear our prayer.

SECOND GHOST
Strong is His arm; it o'er that Power prevailed
Who rose with darkness and His Heavens assailed,
And drove him out, far kindling, as he fell,
Around his head the virgin fires of Hell.
His very eye could clear us all away,
Chase us into the grave, and seal us with the clay.
Hush! breathe not of it, lest for aye He change
To blind obstruction this our nightly range.

FIRST GHOST
Lo! through the churchyard comes a company sweet
Of ghosted infants—who has loosed their feet?
Linked hand in hand, this way they glide along;
But list their softly-modulated song:—

Night The Second

A brooding silence fills the twilight churchyard;
Not even the bat stirs from her cloistered rift,
Nor from her tree the downy-muffled owl,
To break the swooning and bewildered trance.
A crowding stir begins; the uneasy Night
Seems big with gleams of something, restless, yearning,
As if to cast some birth of shape from out
Her hutching loins upon the waiting earth.
The smothered throes are o'er, the birth is out
In glistering ghosts. Thinned and relieved, the air
Lends modulation to their spiritual meanings:—

FIRST GHOST
Disembodied, we on high
Dwell in still serenity.
Name not faculty nor sense,
Where the soul's one confluence
Of light divine, and love, and praise,

From the Lord's unsealèd ways.
Yet we the waiting dust would don,
With our dear bodies clothed upon;
Loving (for He wears the same)
Jesus through our earthly frame:
Then should we sit at Jesus' feet,
Then our Heaven should be complete.
Therefore, for the body's sake,
Oft its thin semblance do we take,
Quick-fashioned from our Paradise,
Thus to revisit where it lies.
And flitting through the night we're fain
To see our mother earth again.

SECOND GHOST

O'er the shadowy vales we go,
O'er the eternal hills of snow,
O'er the city, and its cries
Heard from Belial's nightly sties,
And deserts where no dwellers be,
O'er the land and o'er the sea;
Round the dark, and all away,
Touching on the hem of day.

THIRD GHOST

I had a wife, what earnest-trembling pen
Shall tell her love for me? what words of men?
Spouse of my heart and life! how harsh the pain
To go from thee, and from our children twain!
Unborn unto his sorrowful entail,
The unconscious third could not his loss bewail;
Yet nature reached him when his father died:
Fed on blind pangs within thy widowed side,
And dry convulsive sorrow, bitter food,
He took a deeper stamp of orphanhood,
Than if, life-conscious, he had seen me die,
And wept with many waters of the eye.
This very eve I heard my wife, where she
In saintly calm dwells with our children three;
Their low sweet voices of my name were telling:
Oh how I yearned around their little dwelling!

I could not enter in, I could not make
My presence known, one kiss I could not take!
Yet I rejoice, the Heavenly Watch are keeping
Their nightly vigil o'er the dear ones sleeping.

FOURTH GHOST

Guard the young lambs, ye Angels; Jesus bids,
Who laid His hand on little children's heads!
From Sin defend them, Thou, O Spirit Good!—
None other can—from Sin still unsubdued,
Plague still permitted! Here wide-glorying Crime
Slays half the kingdoms of man's mortal time;
There Pleasure's form belies the ancient pest,
For whom in sackcloth must the worlds be dressed:
She drugs the earth; then by fierce gleams of haste
The false allurements of her eye displaced,
By scorn, by cruel joy her prey to win,
The hoary shape of disenchanted Sin,
Above the nations bowed beneath her spell,
Seals the pale covenant of Death and Hell.

FIFTH GHOST
From the dungeon, from the cave,
From the battle, from the wave,
From the scaffold and its shame,
From the rack, and from the flame,
From the lava's molten stone,
Like a river coming on,
From the Samiel hot and swift,
From the earthquake's closing rift,
From the snow-waste's faithless flaws,
From the monster's rending jaws,
From the famished town, possest
By the blue and spotted pest,
From the lazar-house of pain,
From the mad-house and its chain,—
Day and night, day and night
(Could we hear its gathered might),
What a cry, what a cry,
Prayer, and shriek, and groan, and sigh
(Even the dumb have burst to speech,
In strong yearnings to beseech),
Has gone up to Heaven from earth,
Since that curse of Sin had birth!

SEVENTH GHOST
The glistening infant dies in its first laugh,
Like flower whose fragrance is its epitaph.

SECOND GHOST
Let the sweet fable tell
Of Aphroditè in her rose-lipped shell,
Fresh from the white foam of the morning sea
Into the birth of beauty; ne'er was she

A lovelier emanation to the sight,
Than earth's young virgin in her dewy light.
But see her now!—a faded drooping thing
(When gleam through sleet the violets of the Spring),
Shuddering and shrinking o'er Death's misty jaws,
They suck her down, the shade of what she was!

THIRD GHOST

Yon strenuous youth—a soul of thoughtful duty,
Clothed with heroic beauty—
Look how he scales, so high and clear aloof,
The tops of purpose to the sons of proof.
Death strikes the towering mark,
And slings his name for ever down the dark.

FIRST GHOST

Would the body's death were all
Might the sons of men befall!
But where the spent assault of light
In crystal tremblings dies away
Into the spongy waste of night,
Beyond it I had power to stray:
Far beyond the voice of Thunder,
Through the silent Lands of Wonder,
As they wait the birth of Being,
I was given the power of seeing;
And I saw that baleful place,
For the outcasts of our race.
On the scathed shore, as of a flood
Of fire, a naked creature stood,
Forlorn; and stooping, with his hand
He wrote along the barren sand
Things of remembered earth: His frame
Shook, as he wrote his mother's name.
A noise like coming waves! and lo!
Gleams of a fiery-crested flow!
The molten flood with crowding sway,
Near, nearer, licked those lines away;
Then rising with a sudden roar
(The levelled mist streamed on before),
With horns of flame pushed out, it chased
That being o'er the sandy waste;
Till turning round, with blasphemies
Glaring from out his hollow eyes,
He dared the wrath which, ill defied,
Went o'er him with its whelming tide.
And sights and sounds I cannot name,
Were in that sore possessing flame.

And, ever down from worlds unseen,
(Wrath, wrath beyond what yet hath been!)
Thunderings, and hissings as of rain
Wading through fire, were heard amain.
O place of anguish! place of dread!
Veil the eyes, and bow the head!

SECOND GHOST
A change comes o'er the night; how gracious soft
This light of upper earth to that sad dwelling!
The firmament is full of white meek clouds,
And in them is the moon; slowly she sails,
Edging each one with amber, as she slides
Behind it, and comes out again in glory.
Darkness falls like a breath, and silent brightness
Touches the earth, alternately: how sweet!

THIRD GHOST
But who is this her vigil keeping
O'er a grave?

FOURTH GHOST
The maid is sleeping.
With her old widowed father she
Dwells in her virgin purity,
Young staff of reverence 'neath his weighed years,
Eyes to his dimness, safety to his fears.
And oft when he retires to rest,
She, with her holy thoughts possest,
Comes hither at the shut of day,
To muse beside her mother's clay.
Here once more to muse and weep,
Wearied she hath fallen asleep.

FIFTH GHOST
Filial piety, how sweet!
Kiss her head, and kiss her feet!

SIXTH GHOST
May these kisses, dove, infuse
Power to bear the nightly dews!

FOURTH GHOST
She would fold her arms, and go
To the dark of death below;
Might but a space her mother be
Let up the gladsome day to see.

SIXTH GHOST

But with eternal sanctity
In that mother's soul and eye,
What to her were all the mirth,
Pomp, and glory of the earth?

SEVENTH GHOST

Glistening, solemn, sealed from sin,
She to her spouse at eve comes in.
O that meeting! Does she live?
Milk and honey he would give.
A holy joy, but no excess,
Through her pure body passionless
Thrillingly goes, to hear that voice
Which made her wedded days rejoice.
In silence gazing still on him,
Till tears her spiritual eyes bedim,
Sweet murmurs bless him; round she flings
A glance on old remembered things;
Another gaze on him; and then
She's vanished from the world of men.

FIRST GHOST

Lo! on the maiden's knee the Book of Life!
Kiss every leaf—kiss every wondrous leaf!
The charter of the Paradise we've won,
And Heaven we hope for—kiss each blessed leaf!

SECOND GHOST

Had we, some eighteen hundred years ago,
Been passing through a certain Eastern village,
We might have seen a fair-haired little boy
Stand at his mother's door, in no rude play
Joining His fellows; grave, but holy sweet
Of countenance. Who's that little boy? The God
Who made the worlds—the very God of Heaven!

THIRD GHOST

Love to man, and great salvation!
Wondrous, wondrous Incarnation!

FOURTH GHOST

Ever going to His bed,
At His little feet and head
Looks His mother, laden she
With her burdened mystery;
Still with tears of wonder weeping

O'er the mystic infant sleeping:
He's her son, but He's her Lord!
O the blessed, blessed Word!

FIFTH GHOST
This Book's His Word, and He Himself's the Word!
This Book is the white horses of Salvation,
The chariot this, and this the Conqueror!
Go forth thou Lion-Lamb, far forward bending!
Strike through dark lands with Thy all-piercing eyes!
See, see the shadows break—tumultuous stir,
Masses, abysses! But among them stand,
Pillars of steadfastness, majestic shapes,
Grisly, the Principalities and Powers
Of outer night, wearing upon their brows
Defiance, and the swarthy bloom of Hell.
Go in among them, Thou, go down upon them,
Queller of all dark things, great Head of Flame!
Them with Thy lightnings and compelling thunders
Smite, bow them backward, sweep them to their place!
Burn with Thy wheels! Trample the darkness down
To melting light, and make it Thy clear kingdom!

SIXTH GHOST
Worthy is the Lion-Lamb!
Glory to the great I AM!

SEVENTH GHOST
Sin-spotted youth, world-wearied; difficult age,
Cramped down with stiff-bowed torments; homeless outcasts,
Lying in destitute benumbed caves;
And wanderers reasonless, fantastical,
Gibbering abroad, what time the Moon is hunting
In thin white silence in the shadowy woods;
And stricken creatures in the lazar-house,
Who know no kin, in whom care more than pain
Drinks up the eyes and blood in the night watches,
Or the half draught of suicidal poison
(Remorse and shuddering nature spilt the rest)
Holds its pale quarrel at the heart's red gates;
And they whose hearts are locked up by Despair,
And the key flung into the pit of Hell,—
Even these, all wasted and imperfect natures,
Shall be renewed and finished, and shall walk
Like angels in the white Millennial day,
Day of dead war and of consummate peace:
And that up-going pillared cry of sadness
Shall rise an equal power of praise and gladness.

FIRST GHOST

This little Book the instrument shall be,
Filled with the Spirit; kiss it reverently!

SECOND GHOST

And this virgin bless again,
Free from sin and free from pain!

THIRD GHOST

Her no fabled cestus, wrought
In the magic looms of thought,
Of Gorgon hairs, and coldest gleams
From Dian o'er the morning streams,
And plumes which staid Minerva gave
At midnight from her bird so grave,
Tissued in mystic warp with rays
Plucked from Apollo's head ablaze,
And stings of Wit, whose arrow-tips
In poignant wrath he keenly dips—
A woven dream—encircles round.
A better girdle she has found
In her filial piety,
And that good Book for ever nigh,
In angels, and the Comforter
Whom her dear Lord has sent to her.
Be she where the tempests blow
O'er the North the hail and snow,
Be she where in Southern lands
Hot winds lift the winnowed sands,
Peace with her shall still abide,
The peace that comes from Jesus' side.

FOURTH GHOST

Child of duty, child of honour,
Thus we breathe our wish upon her:
Bless her to Death's earnest gates,
Leading to the separate states;
Bless her to the Judgment-seat,
Bless her to the Heavens complete!

FIFTH GHOST

But ha! I smell the breath of day;
Come away, come away.

And they vanish to the Blest
In the Land of Waiting Rest.

What though no eager yearnings ever pass
With curdled tremblings through the Sea of Glass
Serene, where dwell the spirits of the just;
Yet oft their wishful ghosts revisit here their dust.
Blood-spotted shadows; scarce from darkness won,
The untimely babe that never saw the sun,
Buried at midnight, yearning with dumb strife
For the enlarged capacities of life;
The suicide with stake-impalèd breast,
That in his damnèd crossway cannot rest;
And things of guilt unknown, a thousand ghosts,
A thousand wandering creatures from the coasts
Of outer night, beyond the reach of grace,
With restless flittings fill this burial-place.
Ye sons of living men, first lay aside
Full bread and purple clothing, lust and pride;
And let the clear sense, that ye too must die,
Pierce the fat ear, and purge the filmy eye;
Then hither come, and see these Shapes, and hear,
Sifted from out the dust, their voice of truth severe:—

FIRST GHOST [Rising from a grave]
Mercy! ah! give me mercy! Give me back
My hours of living days—give me but one!
One crystal minute, then! Oh how I'd fill it
With penitential groans, grappling with God,
Bowed by His covenants to hear and pardon!
'Tis past! And the sore pressure lies on me
Of alienation and expected Judgment.
Plaguing my spiritual vision, dooming me
Still more, the image of One crucified,
Ever before me, hanging in the gloom,
So looks at me, piercing me through and through
With His undying patience—O that look!
Come down, thou Meek-face; 'twas not I that did it!
You cannot say 'twas I! Go to the doers
Of the dread literal act; and let them cry
(As cry they must, when the last heat comes on)
For one drop of the water and the blood
From Thy side-wound, to lie one little moment
Upon their fire-curled, cinder-crusted tongues.—
But ha! from out the Judgment-waiting land,
Here comes a Child of Wrath beyond myself.
Hither, thou guiltier Ghost! Knowest thou me?

Thou lord and master of my youthful crimes,
Behold thy scholar! What! thou shivering thing,
Do thy pale skirts of spongy porous mist
Drink up the glimmerings of the lights of night,
Even like mine own? I should have thought thee kneaded
Of leprous crusts of sin, and blistered marle
Baked with the blood of souls, and scurfy dross
From the purged furnaces of Hell, made clear
To the last spirituality of heat
For master sinners. Look upon me, fiend,
Look on thy handiwork, fashioned by thee
Into a thing for Tophet! Was it good
To make me this? My curse go down with thee
Beyond the soundings of extravagant thought!

SECOND GHOST [Advancing]
The old apology for native vice!
Weak thing! as if thy blindly breathing soul
Within thy mother's womb was not engrained
With all thy colours of eternal years!
Our place is wide enough, let's shun each other.

[The SECOND GHOST glimmers away]

FIRST GHOST
He thinks to flee: vain thought! Down he must go!
I too must down! Pitfall, nor den forlorn,
Nor the lone crags of the high-hornèd mountains
Where eagles yelp, jungles, nor sandy lands
Of idle desolation, nor all places
Where the last modesties of nature dwell,
Can hide me from the Power that lets me forth
A little space, to aggravate my doom
By the contrasted sweetness of the earth,
Then draws me back again.—Here are the graves
Of our old house. Would I could gather up
My dust, and take it hence! How shall I bear
The looks of virtuous kindred on that Day,
When summoned I must rise and stand with them,
Even face to face, with all my guilt revealed?
But ha! a new-made grave? Is it my sister's?
Ah! yes, the length and place of it are hers.
My father's and my mother's, long ago
Sunk to the natural level of the earth,
Are hard, and green, and undistinguishable.
But where the spirits of the three? In Bliss,
Let me believe; for I've not known them in

My land of heavy patience. I'm alone
Of all my father's house shut out from Bliss.
Can they be happy when I'm thus shut out?
Oh for the Patriarch's Ladder to come down,
Resting its glory on my mother's dust,
That I might climb the battlements of light,
And be with them for ever!

Help me, my mother, plead for me with Christ!
Stretch down thy dear, dear arms, and take me up;
For I was fashioned in thy holy body;
My father, and my sister, plead for me,
Hang on His wounded side, and plead for me!
The Phantom of his Mother passes by.
Salvation! 'Tis my mother! But she's gone!
Would she but come again, I'd burst my bounds,
And follow her unto the shining doors,
And catch her hand, and she would draw me in!
But ah! she did not speak to me, nor look
Back with regret: 'Twas not my mother, then;
But some false head which the Avenging Power
Built up of crystal air and sunny light,
To mock and plague me.

[The **PHANTOM** again passes by]

She again? 'Tis she!
I'll follow—oh! oh! oh! Perdition has me!
'Tis but the grinning Fiend! See, how he leers
Back through the blasted night! I know thee, Demon,
Practical Liar in impersonations,
As in thy cozening terms and instigations;
Meanest of all created things! But power
Is given him o'er me, and I must go down.

[The **FIRST GHOST** vanishes. The **SECOND GHOST** reappears]

SECOND GHOST
There's no escape! Souls, not yet clothed upon
With semblance, stretching toward the light of life
On the vague shores of Possibility,
Sorrow shall bring you to the birth of blood,
If come you must! Would I had ne'er been born!

[The **SECOND GHOST** vanishes. A strange but short-lived Tempest fills the Churchyard. **THIRD, FOURTH**
FIFTH, and **SIXTH GHOSTS**.]

THIRD GHOST

What Evil Thing so beats about the night,
With dragon wings of tumult and affright?

FOURTH GHOST
By yon trail of sulphurous blue,
Demons here have had to do.
In the livid issue, lo!
Pale and dreadful faces go.

FIFTH GHOST
Wo to the outcasts! Them, nor cunning strings
Melodious, nor soft-stopping pipes, nor all
The sylvan company of sweet-throated birds,
No, nor the very music of the spheres,
Could tune to peace!

[A **SEVENTH GHOST** comes shuddering near]

SEVENTH GHOST

I am that outcast thing!
Ye Powers of Mercy, will ye not yet take
Penance from me on earth? Cut ye it out
From the vast quarries of prodigious sorrow,
Shaping it to my soul, and I will do it.
Be it but on the earth, I care not how
Or where I do it; whether groping through
The barren darkness of the Polar hills,
Or glaring shadowless where the inflamed
Dog of the Firmament, fire-fanged, breating fire,
Bays down with his unmitigated jaws
The panting nations: I will do it there!
Far have I wandered, beating round the bars
Of night, to burst into the boundless day,
Unnoticed; ah! it cannot be, the Power
Of Punishment's too strong and subtle for me,
Curbing me back with his invisible hand.
Wo! wo! my hour is come, and I must down!

[The **SEVENTH GHOST** melts away down into a grave]

FIFTH GHOST
Look! look! oh look! They're gone! Saw ye them not?
Round yon flat table of memorial stone
They seemed to sit, a ghostly company
Of hopeless Ones (judging from their sad faces,
Solemnly sad), there with symbolic handling
Of shadowy elements, trying to renew

The Supper of the Lord, as if they might
Call back the day of mercy and of grace,
And still be Christ's. But full upon them came
A blast from the Evil One, to whom was given
Power o'er their lawless and uncertain rite,
A levelled blast, and whirled them clean away,
Like dry dead leaves, sweeping the naked table
Bare of commemoration. O ye sons
Of living men, lay hold of the blue day
Which yet is yours, hold fast the fleeting night
With struggling prayers—hold them, nor let them go
Till you have made your peace with the Almighty!

SIXTH GHOST
Yon solitary Shade, see how he stands
Aloof—I knew him in the days of earth—
Aloof, alone, and introverted all!
Back, and far back in Memory's inner rooms,
Hung round with haunted glooms, Life's Tragic Sorrows
Act themselves o'er anew, under the eye
Of dread, sole-sitting Conscience.—O that groan!
See how he starts, breaking off all at once
The unfinished trilogies of evolving Guilt,
Shuddering away, self-chased, down into night!

THIRD GHOST
Let us be humbly thankful, we are safe;
Rejoicing humbly, as the little bird
Flies low and coweringly, and with a half
Chirrup of gladness from the fowler's hand.

FOURTH GHOST
Praise to our Elder Brother! But for Him,
No earth had been to us, no life, no Heaven!

FIFTH GHOST
But for His covenanted blood, the Curse
Had killed man's blighted world. The orbs of ether
Spin on the axis of His love. The Bow,
Fashioned of air, and light, and the tears of rain,
Is but the glad reflection of His face,
Graciously pleased. The linnet in the leaves
Christ-chartered sits, while warblings well and bubble
Out from its white-ruffed throat; the dappled fawn
Leaps through the sunny glades, and through the thickets
Bursts, richly powdered with the coloured dust
Of sylvan pith exuberant, and smelling
Of honey-dews, balsams, and dropping gums.

Sleep comes from Him, and peace; the husbandman
Bearing his harvest sheaves, and the blithe shepherd
Piping upon his unmolested hill;
Honey, and wine, and oil; marriage and children;
And all the milky veins of love that run
Branching through nature—all that's fair and good.

SIXTH GHOST

And for the sake of Jesus, God's own Heavens
Are softly set upon a thousand hinges
Of mercy, ever flexible, ever bowing
Flexible downward to the contrite ones.

THIRD GHOST

Afflictions come from Him. The awful Finer
Sits by His furnace pot. The heart of man
Is in the pot—the foul, the stony heart.
Lurid from far, but ever coming nearer,
Fiercer and redder, with its threatened flame,
The heat of Hell burns on the furnace pot.
But all-pervading Love goes quicklier through it,
Melting it down dissolved: The dross is purged
Away, below; and in the liquid metal,
Perfect and pure through suffering, the Finer,
Looking therein, sees His own image clear
Reflected: And the holy workmanship
Of every feature, by His art divine,
He fixes there, never to be effaced.

FIFTH GHOST

Forth stalks the King of Terrors, on his head
The fretted crown of pain; his bony hands
Grasping his sheer cold scythe, down through the field
Of Time he goes, a mower lean and strong,
Mowing his swaths of life. But see, the Babe
Of Bethlehem strikes the crown from off his head,
And breaks his scythe, and casts him into Hell.

SIXTH GHOST

O for the Spirit's day, when Sin and Death
No more shall hurt the people of the Lord!

THIRD GHOST

Hasten Thy day of power, refining Spirit,
Making earth's dwellers like the Saints whose feet
Walk on the terrible crystal.

FOURTH GHOST

Judgment then
Comes unto the sons of men.

FIFTH GHOST
It should be noon; but where's the sun?
The air is stagnant, silent, dun.
Is it eclipse? Is earthquake near?
Nature listens dumb and drear.
That Trump of Doom!
It rends the gloom.
The eagle falls a ruffled heap,
His pinions drowned in endless sleep:
The affrighted horse, half rearing, sinks;
The dull ox, as he stoops and drinks:
The lion in the wilderness
Has crooked his knees to that stern stress.
The quick are changed: the dead arise.
Lo! the Judge is in the skies.
Rejoice, ye Saints! The Saints rejoice
To hear His bliss-awarding voice:
He blesses them, and they are blest
To go into his Heavenly rest.
Wrath for the Wicked! Doomed and driven,
They sink beneath the Eye of Heaven:
Like hurrying draught of bitter cup,
The Eternal Gulf has drunk them up.

SIXTH GHOST
Happy, happy we who dwell
In His love unspeakable,
Fearing not that coming Day,
When heaven and earth shall pass away;
For, from the days of everlasting years,
Ere we were fashioned in the Vale of Tears,
The Lamb—the Judge himself—was pledged to be our stay!

THIRD GHOST
Widening up the eastern skies,
See the pale rim of day arise,
Another day to mortal men,
Toil, and fear, and care again!
Spirit ('tis Thy sacred trust),
Help them, help them, they are dust;
Make them wise, and make them just!
And in great consummation, Dove,
Bring them to our morn above,
Morn of the perpetual day!—
Sister shadows, come away.

[The **GHOSTS** vanish.

www.ingramcontent.com/pod-product-compliance
Lightning Source LLC
Chambersburg PA
CBHW021949040426
42448CB00008B/1318